CLAUDE BOLLING

SONATE POUR GUITARE

for Solo Guitar

ISBN 0-7935-6527-8

HAL•LEONARD™
CORPORATION

7777 W. BLUEMOUND RD. P.O. BOX 13819 MILWAUKEE, WI 53213

SONATE POUR GUITARE

as recorded in *Enchanting Versailles*
Strictly Classical

Part I.
Jazzo-Brasilero

Claude BOLLING

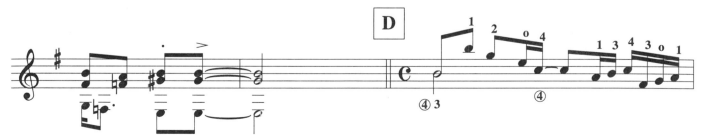

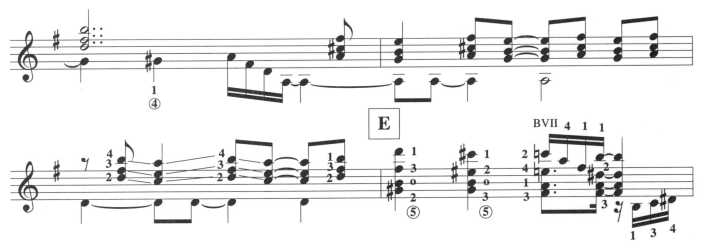

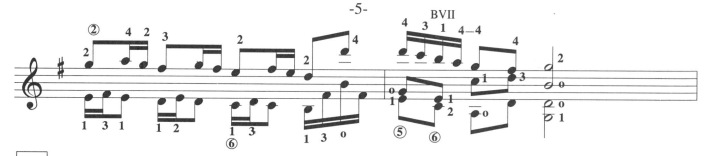

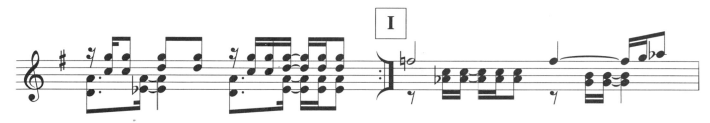

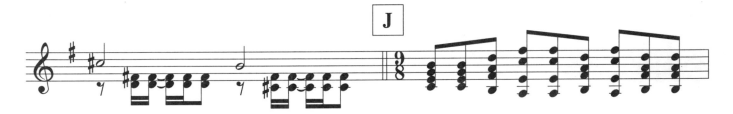

M

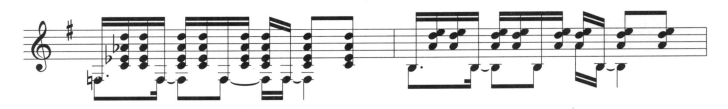

Part II.

Baladina

Claude BOLLING

Ballade Lent ♩ = 54

(2° fois)

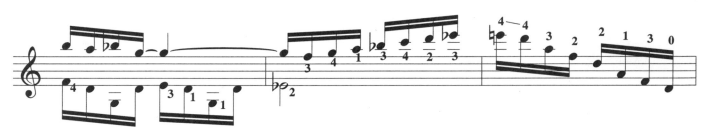

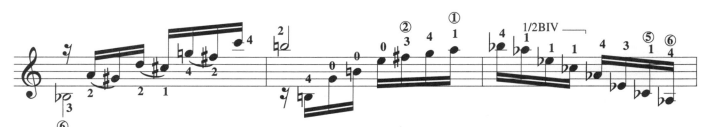

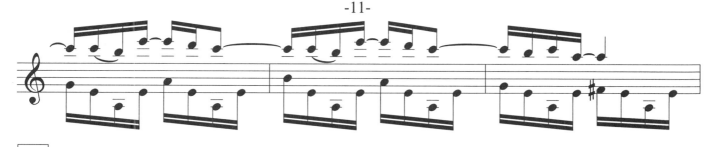

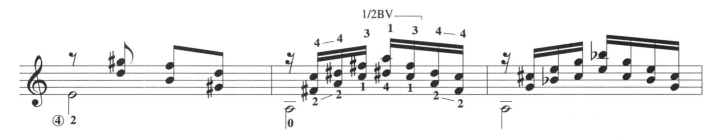

rall. **L** a tempo

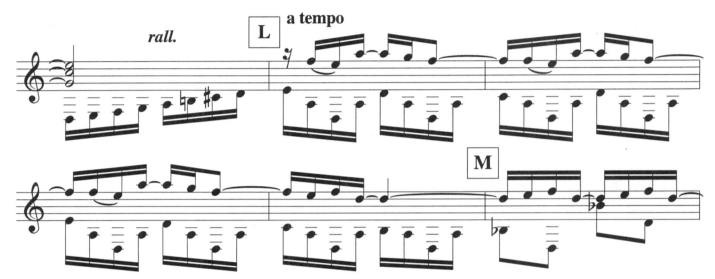

M

N

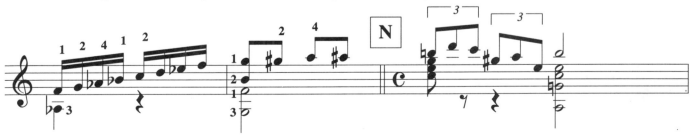

Part III.

Fogoso

Claude BOLLING

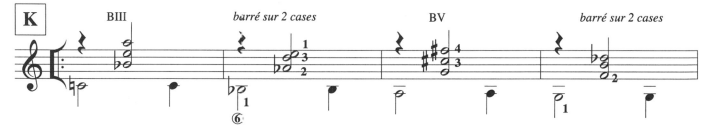

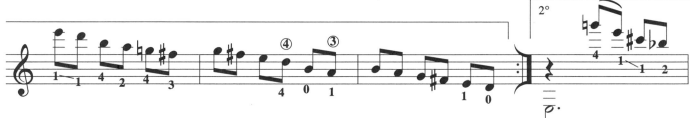

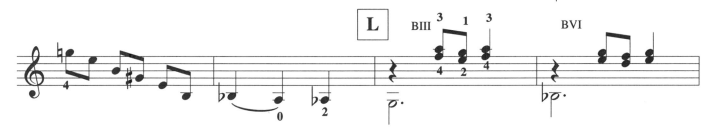

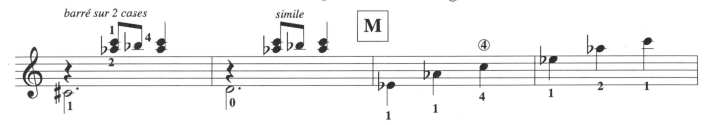

N

O

P

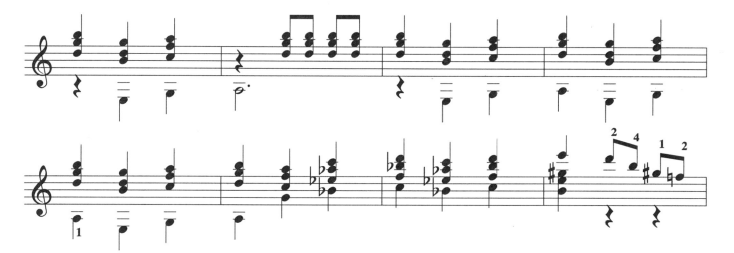